Vegetarianism
for *Teens*

consultant:

Debby Demory-Luce, PhD, RD, LD
Instructor, Department of Pediatrics
USDA/ARS Children's Nutrition Research Center at Baylor
College of Medicine
Houston, Texas

LifeMatters
an imprint of Capstone Press
Mankato, Minnesota

by
Jane
Duden

LifeMatters Books are published by Capstone Press
PO Box 669 • 151 Good Counsel Drive • Mankato, Minnesota 56002
http://www.capstone-press.com

Printed in the United States of America

Library of Congress Cataloging-in-Publication Data
Duden, Jane.
     Vegetarianism for teens / by Jane Duden.
          p.   cm. — (Nutrition and fitness)
     Includes bibliographical references and index.
     ISBN 0-7368-0712-8
     1. Vegetarianism—Juvenile literature. 2. Vegetarian cookery—Juvenile literature. [1. Vegetarianism.
     I. Title. II. Series.
     TX392 .D83 2001
     613.2′62—dc21   00-039092
                                                        CIP

     Summary: Discusses vegetarianism and reasons why some teens choose it; includes information on
     building a healthy vegetarian diet and planning for vegetarian meals and snacks at home and on the

Staff Credits
Rebecca Aldridge, Megan A. Amundson, editors; Adam Lazar, designer and illustrator; Kim Danger, photo
researcher

Photo Credits
Cover: Stock Market Photo/©Paul Barton
©Earthstar Stock Inc., 14
Index Stock Photos/©Image Port, 19, 20; ©Benelux Press, 25; ©BSIP Agency, 26; ©IPS, 33, 44;
©Peter Johansky, 37; ©Zefa, 41
Photo Network/©Esbin-Anderson, 59
Pictor/53, ©Terry Wild Studio, 57
Unicorn Stock Photos/©Jeff Greenberg, 9; ©Martin R. Jones, 51
Uniphoto/©David Stover, 11
Visuals Unlimited/©Mark S. Skalny, 7; ©David Sieren, 31; ©D. Cavagnaro, 47

A 0 9 8 7 6 5 4 3 2 1

Table of Contents

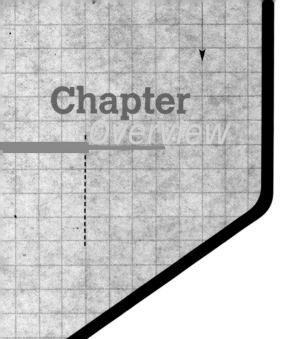

Chapter Overview

- Vegetarianism is a personal choice. Generally, vegetarians do not eat meat. Vegetarianism usually means eating many kinds of plant products such as grains, nuts, fruits, and vegetables. Many types of vegetarians exist, including lacto-ovo vegetarians, lacto vegetarians, ovo vegetarians, and vegans.

- Vegetarianism includes some other alternative diets.

- Vegetarianism sometimes can be a signal that a person has an eating disorder. However, it rarely causes eating disorders.

- A planned vegetarian diet can be a healthy way of eating.

Chapter 1

What Is Vegetarianism?

The Vegetarian Way

Keesha, Age 15

Keesha slid into the booth. "Have you ordered yet?"

"Yes, we got the special pizza. It's loaded with everything," said Trina.

"Did you remember that I don't eat meat?" asked Keesha.

Jackie smiled. "We didn't forget. One half is the special and comes with two kinds of meat. We asked for veggies only on the other half. This way you won't have to pick off the meat."

Trina added, "And we can all enjoy the pizza."

Fast Fact

A little over 1 percent of children and teens are vegetarian. This is according to one poll of students ages 8 to 17.

Being vegetarian is a way of eating. For some teens and adults, it's a whole lifestyle that involves avoiding anything of animal origin. Following a vegetarian diet is a personal choice, as is any diet.

Like Keesha, more teens today than in the past are eating vegetarian meals. They don't eat meat such as hamburgers, pork chops, and steak. Instead, plant foods such as vegetables, fruits, grains, beans, seeds, and nuts make up most of their diet.

Many vegetarians eat dairy products such as milk, butter, and cheese. Some vegetarians include eggs in cooked or baked foods. Some will not eat meat, but sometimes enjoy fish or poultry. Still others will not eat any food that comes from an animal.

Because so many people have chosen a vegetarian diet, many meatless food choices are available. Cookbooks and magazines feature vegetarian cooking. You can find vegetarian cooking shows on television. Restaurants offer tasty vegetarian dishes, and supermarkets sell vegetarian foods. Many Internet sites and public classes teach about vegetarianism.

The Most Common Types of Vegetarians

Not all vegetarians eat the same foods. No single vegetarian diet exists. One teen may eat eggs. Another teen may drink milk. Another may eat fish but no red meat such as beef. Still another may avoid all animal products. Yet all these teens describe themselves as vegetarians. Most vegetarians fall into four groups: lacto-ovo vegetarian, lacto vegetarian, ovo vegetarian, and vegan.

Some vegans and other vegetarians do not wear leather.

Lacto-Ovo Vegetarian

Probably the largest vegetarian group in North America is the lacto-ovo-vegetarian group. *Lacto* means milk, and *ovo* means eggs. Teens in this vegetarian group eat dairy products such as milk and ice cream. They also eat eggs and include vegetables, fruits, grains, and nuts in their diet. They avoid meat, fish, and poultry.

Lacto Vegetarian and Ovo Vegetarian

A second vegetarian group is the lacto-vegetarian group. Like many other vegetarians, they avoid meat, fish, and poultry and eat a lot of plant foods. They also eat dairy foods such as milk, cheese, and yogurt. However, lacto vegetarians do not eat eggs or foods that contain eggs such as many puddings, cakes, and cookies.

The third vegetarian group is the ovo-vegetarian group. These vegetarians eat eggs but do not eat any dairy products.

Vegan

Vegan is the fourth vegetarian group. Vegans do not eat any animal products. They avoid all foods produced by animals, such as honey or milk. Vegans do not eat gelatin, which is made from animal bones. Some vegans as well as some vegetarians take their beliefs further. They do not wear or use leather, silk, or wool products. They do not use down pillows or comforters.

At a Glance

Other vegetarian groups:

Semivegetarians are sometimes called occasional vegetarians or meat restrictors. Like other vegetarians, these teens eat plant foods. On special occasions they may eat fish, but no meat or poultry. Other semivegetarians eat poultry and fish but no meat.

StraightEdge is a subgroup of vegans. These people try to care for the planet and themselves by not using any animal products. They also avoid using drugs and alcohol.

Sheryl and Josh, Age 15

Sheryl walked into the kitchen just as Josh cut a sandwich in half. "That looks good. Can I have a bite?"

"Sure, take half." Josh slid the plate toward Sheryl.

Sheryl looked surprised as she chewed a bite of the sandwich. "This is good! I thought you were a vegetarian, Josh. Along with the tomatoes, onions, and peppers, I see meat."

"I am a vegetarian. That's not meat. It's a portobello mushroom sandwich. Those big, brown mushrooms just seem like meat."

Other Types of Vegetarian Diets

Some teens do not fit into the four common vegetarian groups. Their beliefs may cause them to specialize their diet even more.

Organic Foods

Some vegetarians prefer organic foods that are grown using only natural fertilizers and crop rotation. These people believe that chemical pesticides used to kill bugs are unhealthy. So they choose to eat foods grown organically. They believe that well-balanced soils grow stronger, healthier plants that taste better.

Some vegetarians prefer to eat organic foods that aren't sprayed with chemicals to kill bugs.

Natural Hygiene

Some other vegetarians follow a natural hygiene diet. These people believe that a healthful life includes physical, mental, and emotional health. Following a natural hygiene lifestyle includes getting fresh air and sunshine in addition to eating foods naturally. People who follow this diet do not cook their fruits and vegetables. They eat them only raw or steamed.

Fruitarian Diet

The fruitarian diet is another type of vegetarian diet. Fruitarians do not believe in killing animals or plants for food. They eat only fruits and seeds because these foods fall naturally from plants. The fruitarian diet doesn't provide enough nutrients or calories for good health. Nutrients are the substances in foods that help the body stay healthy and strong.

Macrobiotics

Some people adopt a macrobiotic diet that includes mainly whole grains and vegetables. These people eat certain beans, soups, cooked grains, sea vegetables, and soy-based foods. They also eat a small amount of fruits and fish. Macrobiotic diets limit food variety and fluids. This can result in a diet that falls short of many essential nutrients teens need.

In Canada, females ages 15 to 25 make up the group that most often eliminates meat from its diet.

Who Is a Vegetarian?

More than 12 million American adults say they are vegetarians. Teens, especially teen girls, are the fastest-growing group of vegetarians in North America. This may be because teens are often open to new ideas and like to experiment. In a 1995 Canadian poll, about 16 percent of people ages 12 to 25 were vegetarian. Teenage Research Unlimited ran a 1999 survey of almost 2,000 United States teens. Twenty-two percent said that vegetarianism is popular.

The trend is clear. Many teens think meatless meals are in style. The older the teens, the higher they rated a meatless diet. About 15 percent of college students in the United States eat vegetarian meals and snacks during a typical day.

Vegetarianism Doesn't Mean Eating Disorders

Some experts believe that vegetarianism can be a symptom of eating disorders. These disorders are more about body image beliefs than food. Someone with an eating disorder constantly thinks about food and weight. People with eating disorders need help for their emotional health. Without treatment, an eating disorder can lead to serious health problems and even cause death.

Some teens may use vegetarianism to hide their eating disorder and the lack of high-fat food in their diet. One sign of an eating disorder may be if a person loses weight suddenly after becoming a vegetarian. However, vegetarianism rarely leads to eating disorders.

A well-balanced vegetarian diet can be a healthy eating option for teens.

A Healthy Choice

Vegetarian diets can work well for teens. The American Dietetic Association (ADA) says well-planned vegetarian diets are healthy. Such diets provide teens with adequate, or enough, nutrition and many health benefits.

Points to Consider

- How would you define *vegetarian*?

- Why do you think there are more vegetarians in North America today than in previous years?

- Why do you think teen girls are the fastest-growing group of vegetarians in North America?

- Why do you think girls might be more likely than boys to be vegetarians?

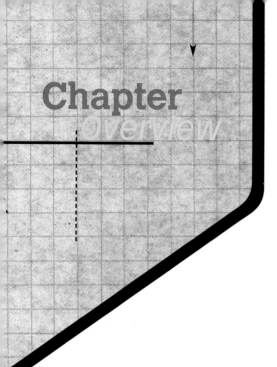

Chapter Overview

- People of various cultures eat many different foods.

- Vegetarian diets have existed for centuries but have become popular in North America only recently.

- There are now many resources for vegetarians.

- Every area of the world has its own unique vegetarian dishes.

Chapter 2

An Old Idea That's New

Pierre, Age 16

Nick and Susan were talking with Pierre, a foreign exchange student. Nick asked Pierre, "What are some things French people eat that Americans don't?"

"Well, I like to eat escargot. They're snails. And some people eat cow tongue and goat brain. Snails are more popular, though," Pierre answered.

"People in France eat frog legs, too, right?" Susan asked.

Pierre nodded. "Yeah, we eat fried frog thighs."

"That's gross!" exclaimed Nick.

Pierre looked at Nick. "I think it's really good. It tastes like fish. I think good food is simply what you are used to."

At one time, tomatoes were thought to be poisonous.

Food Choices Around the World

Food is different around the world. Everyone eats plants, but not everyone eats animals or animal products. Many Americans eat a lot of beef, but most people in India don't because cows are considered sacred. People eat horse meat in Japan and Canada. North Americans don't eat dogs, but dog meat is food in Korea.

Termites, beetles, and other bugs may not be your idea of food. Yet, in parts of Africa, insects provide 60 percent of the protein people eat. Jellyfish and snakes are food to some people. Many people eat hen's eggs, and some people eat fish eggs called caviar.

People have different ideas about plants, too. Asians have eaten tofu and other soybean products for centuries. However, tofu has been slower to catch on in North America. Oats were once fed only to horses. In some countries, corn was food only for livestock. Tomatoes were once thought to be poisonous. You have probably eaten many of these foods without thinking they're strange.

Our Culture Influences Our Diet

Most food choices are learned from a person's culture. For example, haggis is a traditional Scottish dish, but most other people in the world don't eat it. Haggis is meat pudding or sausage with ground lungs and heart from a sheep or calf. This is mixed with oatmeal and boiled in a sheep's stomach.

Favorite foods vary around the world. In China, people buy chicken feet, not popcorn, in movie theaters. Crayfish are dinner in Louisiana, but fishing bait in Michigan. In some states, people like chitlins. This dish is pig intestines fried in fat. Squirrel is a meat treat for some people.

What do you consider food? Not everyone agrees on the answers to this question. Many vegetarians do not consider animals as food. This idea is not recent or unusual.

An Ancient Custom

Vegetarian eating has been a way of life since ancient times. Many people throughout history have been vegetarians.

Vegetarianism has existed in many cultures. It has long been a way of life for some Hindus and Buddhists. They eat no meat because they consider all animal life sacred. Many ancient Greek and Roman philosophers and writers were vegetarians. These people followed a vegetarian diet to live peacefully with animals. Some of these vegetarians believed that eating meat made people dull, slow, or violent.

Throughout history, people in almost every part of the world have followed vegetarian diets. Many people around the world still eat a vegetarian diet. In many places, meat is not plentiful or cheap, so it isn't included in most meals. Instead, eating meat is saved for special occasions.

Vegetarianism Gains Popularity

In the 1600s, vegetarianism gained favor in England. Several religious groups did not eat meat, and soon other people followed vegetarian diets, as well.

The word *vegetarianism* was first used around 1842. It comes from the Latin word *vegetus*, which means lively. In 1847, the Vegetarian Society formed in England. Around 1850, vegetarianism moved across the ocean to North America when three British vegetarians came to the United States. In 1850, the first American Vegetarian Convention was held. As a result of the convention's success, more Americans switched to a plant-based diet.

Vegetarianism also spread throughout Europe. In 1908, the International Vegetarian Union was founded. Today, the union holds meetings every two years in different countries.

Vegetarianism for Teens

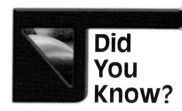

History's famous vegetarians

Clara Barton, American Red Cross Society founder

Charles Darwin, naturalist

Mohandas Gandhi, Indian political leader

George Bernard Shaw, playwright

Percy Bysshe Shelley, poet

Henry David Thoreau, writer

Leo Tolstoy, writer

Recent vegetarian stars

Hank Aaron, baseball player

Prince, singer

Chelsea Clinton, daughter of President Bill Clinton

Janet Jackson, singer

Michael Jackson, singer

k.d. lang, singer

Carlos Santana, musician

Natalie Merchant, singer

Brad Pitt, actor

Natalie Portman, actress

Lisa Simpson, TV character

Liv Tyler, actress

Keenan Ivory Wayans, actor

Vegetarianism Today

Supeen, Age 16

Supeen came to the United States from Thailand. "I am the oldest of 10 kids. In Thailand, my family was poor. We ate mostly white rice, vegetables, and fresh herbs. Banana and mango trees grew nearby, so we had plenty of fruit. We almost never ate meat because it cost too much.

"Even eggs were expensive. I remember one time when my mother traded with a neighbor to get some eggs. We fried them and then split them into little pieces and stirred them into a big bowl of rice. I still remember how good that tasted.

"I'm still a vegetarian, even after moving to the United States. It's a way of life for me."

For centuries, many people in Asia and India have followed a vegetarian diet. Today, that trend is changing, and people in these regions are eating more animal products than before.

The opposite is true in North America and Europe. In these areas, animal products were priced so that most people could afford them. For this reason, a diet centered around meat was common. However, in the 1970s, this started to change. That's when the animal rights movement began and people turned to vegetarian eating. People talked about meatless eating and solving world hunger. Many people saw vegetarianism as the answer to many environmental and social problems.

The magazine *Vegetarian Times* began in 1974. Today, thousands of people read this and other vegetarian magazines. Bookstores and libraries offer many vegetarian books, and many Internet sites have health information and recipes for vegetarians.

Chinese noodles with soy beef is one example of a vegetarian meal that comes from Asia.

Wide World of Vegetarianism

Every area of the world has its own vegetarian dishes. Many of these foods are now common in North American supermarkets. Ethnic, or cultural, restaurants and supermarkets can be found in many cities and offer a variety of foods.

Foods From Asia

Vegetarianism is an ancient tradition among Asian people. In Japan, Korea, and China, rice or noodles are the main part of a meal. Southeast Asian countries such as Vietnam and Thailand also feature rice or noodles in their meals.

Asian diets include soy and other bean products. Soybeans are used to make many foods, including soy sauce that flavors many dishes. Soybeans also are used to make tofu, which looks like soft cheese. Tofu is high in protein and can be eaten different ways.

Many Asians eat vegetables regularly, even for breakfast. Vegetables commonly used include bean sprouts, mushrooms, radishes, and different cabbages such as bok choy. Cooks often flavor meals with garlic, ginger, and pepper. Dessert usually is fresh fruit.

Foods From the Mediterranean

Greece, Italy, and Spain are countries along the Mediterranean Sea. The people of these countries often rely on pasta, rice, and breads for their meals. Many of these people also eat beans, cheeses, and lots of vegetables.

Bulgur is a "rice" often used in the Middle East. It's part of this vegetable and bulgur stew.

Most Mediterranean foods are cooked in olive oil. Herbs such as rosemary, basil, and oregano often are added to dishes. Garlic, lemon, and mint are popular, too.

The Middle East and North Africa lie across the Mediterranean Sea from Greece, Italy, and Spain. Rice and breads are the staples, or main foods, in the Middle East and North Africa. The rice of the Middle East actually is a cracked wheat called bulgur. The Middle Eastern diet also includes many beans and vegetables.

Foods From India

For the past several hundred years, India has had a tradition of vegetarianism. Rice and wheat are the main foods of India. People eat many kinds of flat breads. Legumes also are a major part of the Indian diet. A legume is a plant with seeds that grow in pods. Legumes are full of protein. Lentils and split peas are the most commonly used legumes.

People in India also eat many kinds of fresh fruits and vegetables. Chutneys, or sauces made from ground or chopped fruits and vegetables, add flavor to some Indian foods.

The best-known seasoning used in many Indian dishes is curry powder. Garlic, mint, and parsley also are popular. Yogurt often cools spicy Indian foods.

"My Lebanese neighbor taught me how to make my favorite salad. It's called tabbouleh and is made with bulgur, parsley, onions, mint leaves, and lemon juice. I love a big bowl of tabbouleh along with crackers and cheese."—Jason, age 13

Foods From Mexico, Central America, and South America

Colorful beans play an important role in the dishes of Mexico, Central America, and South America. Pinto, red, and black beans are especially popular. Many people from these regions also eat a lot of tortillas and rice. Tortillas are flat breads often made from corn. They can be eaten alone or stuffed with vegetables and beans. People may add salsa on top.

Salsas made from finely chopped tomatoes, chili peppers, and onions add zest to many Latin American dishes. Hot chilies, garlic, cilantro, and limes are added to many dishes, too.

Plantains are another staple. These fruits look like bananas but are used like vegetables. Plantains and other tropical fruits such as mangoes and papayas give meals color and sweetness.

Points to Consider
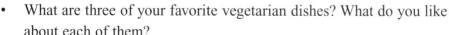

- What influences your diet?

- What are three of your favorite vegetarian dishes? What do you like about each of them?

- Is your family willing to try new ethnic dishes? Why or why not?

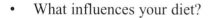

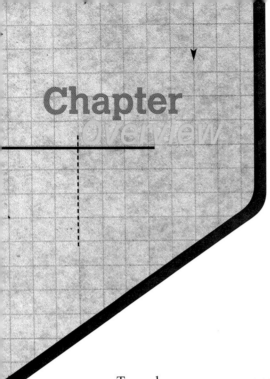

Chapter
Overview

- Teens have many reasons for being vegetarian.

- Some teens think it's wrong to eat animals.

- Some teens think vegetarianism can help relieve world hunger.

- Some teens avoid eating meat to help the environment.

- Religion and health are other reasons some teens choose a vegetarian diet.

Chapter 3

Why Eat Vegetarian?

Robert, Age 14

"What's for dinner, Dad?" Robert asked as he dropped his schoolbooks onto the kitchen counter.

"We're having chicken tonight."

Robert shook his head. "Don't make any for me. I'm not eating meat anymore."

"But chicken isn't meat. Beef is meat," Robert's dad said.

"I won't eat anything that had a face," said Robert.

Teens usually make their own choices about which foods to eat. Today, more teens than ever before are choosing not to eat meat. Each vegetarian has a different reason for this choice. Many teens say they are vegetarians for environmental reasons and because they love animals. Teens often choose vegetarianism for one reason, such as animal rights. Later they may adopt other reasons, such as health, too.

"I'm a vegetarian. I think it's better for my health, the environment, and animals, too. I feel better about myself when I don't eat meat."
—Maggie, age 14

Concern for Animals

Many teens become vegetarians because they love animals. These teens may feel that it's painful and cruel to kill animals for food. They believe that being a vegetarian shows respect for other forms of life. To them, being a vegetarian means that one less person buys animal products, creating less demand for meat. Vegetarians hope this also means that fewer animals are killed for food.

Vegans and some vegetarians also avoid animal products in clothing, makeup, and other items. The animal parts used in these products often come from animals that were killed for food. By taking their beliefs one step further, these vegetarians lessen the demand for all animal products. They believe that fewer animals will be killed if no animal parts are needed. They also do not buy or use products that are tested on animals.

World Hunger

Some vegetarians believe vegetarianism can help stop world hunger. Raising animals for food requires huge amounts of food and water. It takes 15 pounds (6.8 kilograms) of grain to produce 1 pound (.5 kilograms) of meat. Many vegetarians feel that this grain should be used to feed people instead. Then, fewer people would be hungry.

Some vegetarians believe that land is better used for raising crops than animals. They feel that using land to raise plants would provide more food for more people. A farmer can raise 250 pounds (113.4 kilograms) of beef on 1 acre (4046.9 square meters) of land. That same amount of land could produce 50,000 pounds (22,680 kilograms) of tomatoes. Or, it could produce 40,0000 pounds (18,144 kilograms) of potatoes or 30,000 pounds (13,608 kilograms) of carrots.

Some teens choose vegetarianism because they don't feel animals should be killed for food.

The Environment

Some teens become vegetarians to help preserve natural resources. Fewer resources are used to grow plants for food than to raise animals for meat. Growing plants to eat uses much less land, water, and energy.

Some teens are upset that rain forests are cleared to raise animal feed or cattle. They feel that too much land has been lost already this way. They are concerned that native peoples may lose their home and that plants and animals may become extinct.

These teens also choose meatless diets to reduce the demand for meat. This can mean less land is cleared for cattle. More rain forests may stay intact, and air and water supplies may remain unharmed.

Binh, Age 15

Binh moved to America from Vietnam. "My family practices Buddhism. In Buddhism, there is no supreme power or leader. People are guided by groups of monks. My uncle is a monk. He's a strict vegetarian. He believes all animals have a soul. So, he eats mostly fruits, vegetables, and rice."

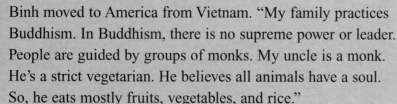

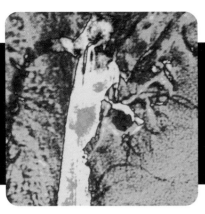

A vegetarian diet may protect against blocked arteries.

Religious or Spiritual Beliefs

Vegetarianism is part of many religions. Some religions require that people not eat meat. Many Buddhists, Hindus, Jains, and people of other Eastern religions are vegetarians. Seventh Day Adventists are one of the largest vegetarian groups in North America.

Health

Some teens believe that eating meat can harm the human body. Vegetarian diets tend to be lower in fat and higher in fiber than diets with meat. Fiber is a substance that aids digestion. Having a diet low in fat and high in fiber follows the United States government's program on healthy eating. This program is called the Dietary Guidelines for Americans.

Because a vegetarian follows these guidelines, some conditions linked to diet are less common among vegetarians. These include obesity, or being seriously overweight, and some cancers. Osteoporosis is a condition that causes bones to become fragile and break easily. Osteoporosis may occur less commonly among vegetarians than among those who eat meat.

A diet without meat can help guard against some serious health problems such as diabetes and high blood pressure. Diabetes is a disease in which a person has too much sugar in the blood. A meatless diet also can protect against arteriosclerosis. In this condition, arteries become blocked, and blood cannot reach the brain or heart. Death can result. A well-planned vegetarian diet helps prevent these and other diseases. Vegetarian diets also can help people who already have these conditions to control them.

Fast Fact

The National Cancer Institute has identified about three dozen plant foods that protect against cancer. These foods include garlic, onions, soybeans, carrots, citrus fruits, broccoli, tomatoes, and peppers. Brown rice, oats, whole wheat, cucumbers, berries, basil, and sage protect against cancer, too.

José, Age 16

José became a vegetarian at age 12. "My dad had surgery for colon cancer. Afterward, his doctor told him not to eat red meat and to eat more whole-grain foods. My mom and I stopped eating red meat to help my dad. I also wanted to try lowering my risk of colon cancer, so I became a vegetarian. My mom became a vegetarian at age 51. Now, our meals have changed to fit our diet. We serve chicken to my dad about once a week."

Other Reasons for Vegetarianism

Some teens simply do not like the taste of meat. They prefer the flavors and mixtures of vegetables and grains in vegetarian dishes. Other teens grow up in vegetarian families. These teens are used to eating meals without meat and that are based on plant foods.

Points to Consider

* How do you feel about vegetarianism?

* Which reason or reasons for becoming a vegetarian make the most sense to you?

* What other reasons have you heard for becoming a vegetarian?

* How do you react when you hear that someone is a vegetarian?

* How can your diet today affect your health in the future?

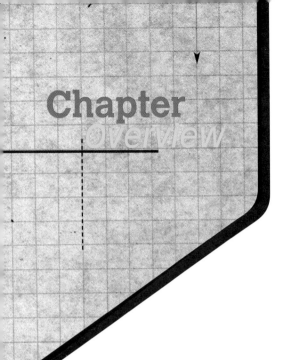

Chapter Overview

- A diet without meat can supply the proper nutrition teens need.

- It's important that vegetarians pay special attention to the nutrients they need. These include protein, calcium, iron, vitamins D and B_{12}, and zinc.

- Vitamin supplements usually aren't necessary for vegetarians who follow a well-planned diet.

- Canada and the United States provide food guides that can help teen vegetarians plan a well-balanced diet.

Chapter 4

Building a Healthy Vegetarian Diet

Many health experts agree that vegetarian diets are healthy. That's because most vegetarian diets follow the Dietary Guidelines for Americans and the Canadian Food Guide to Healthy Eating. Well-planned vegetarian meals and snacks can supply all the necessary nutrients a person needs. Animal foods aren't necessary for healthy eating.

Nutrients You Need

Following a vegetarian diet takes nutritional awareness. Nutrition is food that contains substances the body needs to stay healthy and strong. Nutrients in food provide the body with nutrition.

Everyone needs carbohydrates, proteins, fats, vitamins, minerals, and water, which all are nutrients. Carbohydrates provide the body with energy. Proteins provide energy, too. They also build and repair body tissue. Fats not only provide energy but also help the body use vitamins. Different vitamins help specific parts of the body. In general, vitamins are good for the cells and help blood to clot. Minerals help keep body fluids balanced. These elements found in the earth also add structure to body tissue. Water is important because it's used in almost everything the body does. The teen body is 60 to 70 percent water.

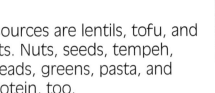

Myth: You can get protein only from animal products.

Fact: Good protein sources are lentils, tofu, and low-fat dairy products. Nuts, seeds, tempeh, peas, whole-grain breads, greens, pasta, and corn are all rich in protein, too.

Teens who don't eat meat or dairy must choose their meals and snacks with care. In most diets, meat, fish, and poultry are major sources of B vitamins and the mineral iron. Meat and shellfish are major sources of another mineral—zinc. Teens who don't eat meat must replace these missing nutrients by eating other foods that contain them. That isn't hard to do with all the nutritious plant foods available.

The key to a healthy diet is to eat a wide variety of foods. Vegetarian or not, everyone needs to eat fruits, vegetables, and plenty of leafy green vegetables. Everyone should eat lots of whole-grain products, nuts, seeds, and beans. Sweets and fatty foods should be eaten only once in a while.

Vegetarian Teens and Protein

Kay, Age 14

Sarah sat by Kay in the cafeteria. "Kay, you never have meat in your sandwiches or on your pizza. Don't you get hungry for meat?" Then Tony added, "People are supposed to eat meat. It's the only way to get protein. Don't you know that?"

Kay pointed to her sandwich. "This whole-grain bagel has protein. The peanut butter on it has protein, too. The beans in my soup contain protein. I guess you didn't know that."

Collard greens are a good source of calcium.

People may worry that vegetarians do not receive enough protein. A carefully selected vegetarian diet can easily meet a teen's protein needs. This means eating a variety of foods high in protein and with enough calories to maintain a healthy weight.

Diet Checklist for Vegetarian Teens

It's important for vegetarian teens to pay special attention to several nutrients that may be lacking in their diet. This list can serve as a guide.

- **Keep track of the foods you eat that are rich in calcium.** This mineral is important for strong bones and teeth. Calcium helps blood to clot, muscles to contract, and nerves to work. Food labels can tell you how much calcium is in a serving of food you are eating.

  Collard greens, broccoli, kale, low-fat dairy products, and turnip greens all contain calcium. Soy milk, soy cheese, and tofu are not naturally rich in calcium, but many kinds are fortified with calcium. That means calcium has been added to them. Other foods that may be fortified with calcium include juices, breakfast bars, and cereals.

Combining foods rich in iron and vitamin C can increase the amount of iron your body absorbs. Try these food teams:

- Strawberries and iron-fortified cereal
- Orange juice and oatmeal with sesame seeds on top
- Tomatoes and cooked dried beans
- Grapefruit juice and a peanut butter sandwich on iron-fortified, whole-grain bread
- A salad tossed with broccoli, red bell peppers, and sesame seeds
- Sliced kiwi with whole-grain toast

- **Look for vitamin D.** This vitamin helps your body use calcium. It's good for bones and teeth. Daily sunshine provides enough vitamin D for many teens in sunny climates. Teens who live in northern regions may need to get vitamin D from foods. Teens who have dark skin or use sunscreen may need to do so as well.

  Vitamin D is added to cow's milk and fortified soy milk or rice milk. You also can get vitamin D from fortified breakfast cereals and vitamin supplements.

- **Eat foods that contain iron and vitamin C.** The mineral iron is stored as part of hemoglobin in the blood. Hemoglobin brings oxygen to cells and carries carbon dioxide away from cells. Too little iron in the diet can cause one type of anemia. People with this condition do not have enough hemoglobin in the blood. This may cause them to feel weak or tired all the time. Many teens, especially girls, do not get enough iron.

Eating iron-fortified cereal and kiwi together can help your body to increase the amount of iron it absorbs.

Careful vegetarian teens can get enough iron because many plant foods contain iron. However, plant foods usually contain less iron than meats do, and this iron is less readily absorbed. Good plant sources of iron are whole-grain foods and iron-fortified breads, cereals, and pastas. Broccoli, spinach, collard greens, dried beans, dried fruits, seeds, and tofu are good sources of iron, too. It helps to eat these foods together with foods that contain vitamin C. That's because vitamin C helps the body to absorb the iron from plant sources. Citrus fruits, strawberries, green peppers, kiwi, broccoli, and tomatoes are good sources of vitamin C.

- **Be sure to get vitamin B$_{12}$.** Animal products are the only natural food sources of vitamin B$_{12}$. A diet that includes dairy products or eggs can provide teens with enough vitamin B$_{12}$. Other foods such as some cereals and fortified soy milks contain B$_{12}$. Meat substitutes called analogues also have B$_{12}$. Only vegans may need to add vitamin B$_{12}$ to their diet in the form of a supplement.

Vitamin Supplements

Vitamin and mineral supplements usually aren't necessary for vegetarians to receive all the nutrients they need. If you do decide to take a vitamin and mineral supplement, check the label. Many labels now state if the supplement is suitable for vegetarians. Some labels say that the supplement contains no animal ingredients or that it's dairy-free. Check with a doctor before taking a supplement. This is because too much of certain vitamins and minerals can do more harm than good.

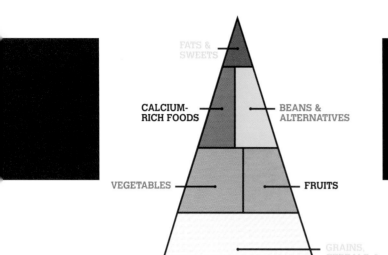

FATS & SWEETS

CALCIUM-RICH FOODS

BEANS & ALTERNATIVES

VEGETABLES

FRUITS

GRAINS, CEREALS, & PASTAS

The Vegetarian Food Guide Pyramid can help you choose a healthy and balanced diet.

Food Guides for Vegetarians

Gerald, Age 15

Gerald's sister watched him tape a magazine page to the refrigerator.

"What's that?" his sister asked.

"This is the Vegetarian Food Guide Rainbow," Gerald said. "Now that I'm vegan, I don't eat meat, dairy, or eggs. This guide will remind me how much and what kind of food to eat each day. I'm going to keep it on the refrigerator where I can see it."

Canada and the United States have guides to help teens plan a healthy diet. Both countries have specific vegetarian food guides that tell the kinds and the amounts of vegetarian food to eat daily. These guides can help vegetarian teens plan healthy meals and snacks.

Food guides show a range of servings for each food group. Count your servings to fit how active you are. Gender, or sex, as well as age and size also affect the number of servings each person needs.

Get the Servings You Need

The right number of servings provides the nutrients you need. Ten servings may sound like a lot, but a serving usually is smaller than most people think. Servings can add up quickly. By choosing a variety of foods within each group every day, you'll have interesting, tasty, nutritious meals and snacks. The following chart lists recommended daily servings and some serving sizes.

A Vegetarian Teen's Food Guide

Food Group	Number of Servings	Serving Sizes
Grains, breads, cereals	8 to 10	1 slice bread, ¼ bagel, ½ hamburger bun or English muffin
		1 ounce (30 grams) dry cereal
		½ cup (115 grams) cooked rice or pasta
Leafy green vegetables	1 to 2	½ cup (115 grams) cooked or 1 cup (225 grams) raw leafy vegetables
Other vegetables	3	½ cup (115 grams) cooked or 1 cup (225 grams) raw vegetables
Fruits	2 to 4	½ cup (115 grams) or 1 piece fresh fruit
		¾ cup (180 milliliters) fruit juice
		¼ cup (60 grams) dried fruit

If you drink cola, tea, or coffee, it's better to drink them between meals rather than with meals. That's because of tannins found in coffee, tea, and cola. Plants produce tannins to protect the outer and inner plant tissues. Tannins combine with iron and decrease the iron your body can absorb.

Food Group	Number of Servings	Serving Sizes
Legumes/meat substitutes	2 to 3	½ cup (115 grams) cooked beans
		4 ounces (115 grams) tofu
		2 tablespoons (30 grams) peanut butter
		2 tablespoons (30 grams) nuts or seeds
		1 egg or 2 egg whites
Nuts and seeds	1 to 2	2 tablespoons (30 grams) nuts, seeds, or nut butters
Milk or milk substitutes and calcium-fortified foods	4 to 6	1 cup (240 milliliters) milk, soy milk, or yogurt
		1½ ounces (45 grams) cheese or soy cheese
		1 cup (240 milliliters) calcium-fortified juice
Fats and sweets	Use sparingly	1 teaspoon (5 milliliters or grams) vegetable oil, margarine, or butter
		1 tablespoon (15 grams) salad dressing or mayonnaise

Polenta and beans is one of Chris's favorite vegetarian dishes.

Chris, Age 13

"A lot of people think a vegetarian eats only salad for every meal. That's not true. I eat all kinds of different foods. At the grocery store, I find interesting foods such as polenta, portobello mushrooms, and seitan. These foods give me ideas for new dishes to invent. I love to find new kinds of noodles, pasta, and rice. My latest find is pasta made from amaranth. For me, the best part of being a vegetarian is trying new things."

Points to Consider

- Why is variety important in a vegetarian teen's diet?

- How could one of the food guides improve your diet?

- What information on food labels can help you make wise food choices?

- Compare your daily diet to the Food Guide Pyramid or Rainbow. Do you come close to eating the daily recommended servings of the food groups? How could you make your diet even better?

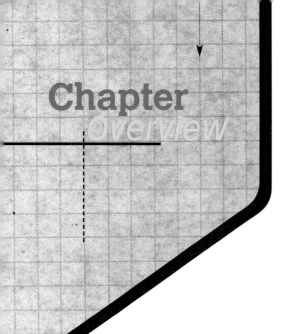

Chapter Overview

- Whole grains, legumes, and soy products are a big part of vegetarian diets.

- Many new vegetarian foods appear in stores every year.

- Vegetarian meat substitutes may look and taste like meat.

- Vegetarian recipes can be easy, fun, and delicious.

Chapter 5

Meal Planning at Home

Plan for Plant Foods

Vegetarians can get the nutrients they need from plant foods. Whole grains, legumes, and soy products are important foods in a vegetarian diet. If you know what these foods are, you can add variety to your diet.

Wheat, corn, rice, oats, rye, millet, and barley are examples of grains. Each grain comes in a different form. Grains can be made into cereal, flour, bread, pasta, and more. Whole-grain foods have many nutrients and are healthier than foods made with refined, or processed, flour. This is because the process that changes grains into flour takes away the whole-grain kernel. This part of the whole grain contains many of its nutrients.

Legumes are plants rich in protein. They include beans, peas, lentils, and black-eyed peas. Black beans, lima beans, kidney beans, and chickpeas (also called garbanzo beans) are legumes, too. Pinto beans, mung beans, white beans, split peas, and soybeans also are legumes. This wide variety means many choices for planning meals with legumes.

Food combinations that include complete proteins:

Beans and rice

Peanut butter on whole-grain bread

Cereal with milk

Include New Ingredients

Many new vegetarian foods appear often. Some new foods are boxed or frozen meals. Many are new types of vegetables or fruits. Watch for new foods that can add variety and nutrition to your diet.

Soy Products

Many new foods made from soybeans appear each year. Soy products have gained popularity as people have learned how healthful they are. The protein in soy is the most complete protein of any vegetable source. A complete protein has all the amino acids the body needs. Soy is the only plant source of complete protein. All other plant foods that have protein contain only some amino acids. These foods need to be eaten with other plant foods to provide complete protein. For this reason, vegetarians often make soy foods a big part of their diet.

Soy milk is made from cooked soybeans. It's used in the same ways as cow's milk. It's a good idea to choose soy milk that is fortified with calcium and vitamin D. You also can find soy cheese, spreads, yogurts, frozen desserts, and even a soy "sour cream." These all are eaten and used in the same manner as the dairy product they are similar to. Think of these soy products when you plan meals and snacks.

Tofu is made from curdled soy milk. This process is similar to how cheese is made. Tofu is formed into soft cakes to use in place of meat. It is inexpensive and easy to prepare. Tofu provides lots of protein with less unhealthy saturated fat and cholesterol than meat does. Too much cholesterol can block blood vessels and blood flow to the heart and brain. This blockage eventually can cause heart attack and stroke. Eating too much saturated fat often leads to high cholesterol levels in the blood.

Tofu can be used in many different ways.

You usually can find two types of tofu in supermarkets or health food stores. Blocks of tofu packed in water are in the refrigerator section. A second kind of tofu comes in aseptic packages that protect the tofu from disease-causing organisms. This tofu is found on grocery store shelves. This type of tofu doesn't need to be refrigerated until you open it. Once opened, all tofu should be stored in the refrigerator.

Stephan and Cara, Age 16

Stephan watched Cara unwrap her pita sandwich and fruit salad. "I'm becoming a vegetarian," he said. "What do you think I should know?"

Cara smiled. "That's easy! For one thing, don't eat just vegetables. Some people think that's all we eat. They forget about other foods such as pasta and rice. You could try seitan or a meat substitute called TVP®. When you add boiling water to TVP, it soaks up the water and looks just like meat. I know people who love tofu, but I'm not crazy about it. The point is, don't be afraid to try new things."

Meat Substitutes

Meat analogues are meat substitutes made from wheat or soy. They imitate sausages, hot dogs, hamburgers, or chicken patties. Tofu hotdogs, tempeh, seitan, tuno, and TVP (textured vegetable protein) are meat analogues. All have the protein found in meats. They may even look and taste like meat when cooked. New meat analogues appear at grocery stores regularly. Try various brands, and you may find some you like.

Broccolini™ baby broccoli is a new vegetable. This cross between broccoli and Chinese kale looks more like asparagus than broccoli. It is edible from flower to stem. One serving of broccolini contains the daily requirement of vitamin C!

Tips for Planning Easy Meals

Here are some tips for planning meals and snacks.

- Follow a food guide when you plan meals and snacks. (See Chapter 4.)

- Think of vegetables or grains as the stars of your meals.

- Check out the recipes for your family meals. You often can use them to make your own vegetarian dishes. For example, maybe your mom makes a casserole that you really like. You can make a casserole with all the same ingredients, but use tofu instead of meat.

- Cook extra servings when making pasta or rice. Then, put the extra servings in the refrigerator for your next meal. Chop extra carrots or onions when you make stir-fry, and use the rest in soup the next day.

- Save leftovers. It's fun to change them for tomorrow's meal. Use salad to stuff pita bread, or add noodles to leftover vegetarian chili.

- Keep some packaged foods on hand for days when you're short on time.

- Get recipe ideas from the Internet and from friends.

"All this cooking for myself has turned into a great hobby. Cooking is a talent I didn't know I had. My friends come over, and we all cook together."—Jared, age 16

Andy and Ladelle, Age 14

Andy and Ladelle set down their books on the kitchen table. "I'm starved," said Ladelle. "Let's make some hummus. We can eat it as dip with carrots and celery."

"Okay, I'll try it," answered Andy. "Your veggie food is a little weird, but I'm hungry."

Ladelle made the hummus while Andy cut up some carrots and celery. In 10 minutes they were eating. "This is good! I like the garlic flavor," Andy said.

Ladelle nodded. "I'll take the rest in my lunch tomorrow. My favorite sandwich is hummus in pita bread. I'll grate some of those carrots to put in it, too."

Recipes to Try

Vegetarian teens don't have to settle for the family's side dishes. They don't have to be chefs. Simple recipes and good ingredients help even a beginning vegetarian to make healthy and interesting meals. With practice, you can invent your own dishes to impress family and friends.

Hummus is a Middle Eastern dip made from garbanzo beans.

Easy Hummus

Ingredients

1 can organic garbanzo beans (about 2 cups or 450 grams), drained and rinsed

¼ cup (60 grams) tahini (sesame butter, sold near peanut butter in stores)

2 tablespoons (30 milliliters) olive oil (optional)

2 to 3 cloves garlic, minced (chopped finely)

About 2 tablespoons (30 milliliters) lemon juice (usually from ½ of a lemon)

Water

Directions

Mix all ingredients except water together in a blender or food processor. Add water to reach desired thickness. You may want hummus thick for pita spread, or thin as a sauce for veggie burgers. Serve hummus as dip with baby carrots and other fresh vegetables. Or, spread on pita bread cut into triangles.

Tempeh Reubens

Ingredients

1 8-ounce (225-gram) package tempeh
8 slices pumpernickel bread
Thousand Island dressing (see following recipe)
½ cup (115 grams) sauerkraut

Directions

Cut tempeh into four equal pieces that resemble thin rectangles. Heat pieces in pan until brown on one side. Then flip and heat until brown on the other side. Place each piece on a slice of pumpernickel bread. Top the tempeh with sauerkraut and Thousand Island dressing. Then put another piece of pumpernickel over the tempeh, sauerkraut, and dressing to make a sandwich. Then, fry in a nonstick pan as you would to make a grilled cheese sandwich. Makes four servings.

Thousand Island Dressing

Ingredients

2 tablespoons (30 grams) fat-free soy mayonnaise
1 tablespoon (15 grams) ketchup
1 tablespoon (15 grams) pickle relish

Directions

Mix ingredients together in a bowl. Use on sandwiches or salads. Makes eight servings.

"I don't use dairy products. That's why I read about good sources of calcium. Now I snack on soynuts, figs, and almonds, or I drink a glass of orange juice that has calcium. Tahini is a sesame paste I just discovered. I love tahini on a bagel."
—Dwayne, age 15

Sesame Baked Tofu

Ingredients

⅓ cup (75 milliliters) toasted sesame oil

¼ cup (60 milliliters) tamari or soy sauce

1 tablespoon (15 milliliters) rice or cider vinegar

2 garlic cloves, minced

¼ cup (60 grams) chopped onion

2 teaspoons (10 grams) grated fresh ginger

⅓ cup (75 milliliters) water

1 pound (450 grams) tofu, cut into slices ½-inch (1.5-centimeters) thick

Directions

Preheat oven to 375 degrees Fahrenheit (F) (190 degrees Celsius [C]). Combine all ingredients except tofu in a large shallow baking dish. Place tofu slices in the dish, turning them over so all sides get dipped in the liquid and seasonings. Bake for 20 minutes. Turn slices over and bake for 20 minutes more or until the tofu absorbs all the liquid. Makes four servings.

Kale provides the body with calcium.

Roasted Potatoes and Kale

Ingredients

2 or 3 Yukon Gold potatoes, scrubbed and cut into 1-inch
(2.5-centimeter) chunks

1 yam or sweet potato, peeled and cut into 1-inch (2.5-centimeter)
chunks

1 yellow onion, chopped

1 bunch kale, chopped and steamed for 5 minutes

3 tablespoons (45 milliliters) olive oil

¼ teaspoon (1 gram) nutmeg

½ teaspoon (2 grams) rosemary

Salt and pepper to taste

Directions

Preheat oven to 375 degrees F (190 degrees C). Place all vegetables in
a 3-quart or 3-liter casserole dish. Combine olive oil and spices. Stir
this mixture into the vegetables. Cover and bake about 30 minutes.
Remove cover and roast for 15 minutes more. Makes six servings.

Points to Consider

- Why is it important for vegetarian teens to plan the foods they eat?

- What soy products do you eat? Would you like to try soy products?
  Why or why not?

- How could you add tofu to your meals?

- What are some ways you could find vegetarian recipes?

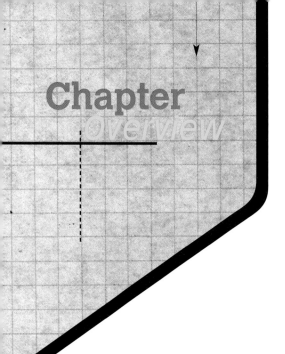

Chapter *Overview*

- Snacks are important sources of energy and nutrients for teen vegetarians. Teens can make lots of vegetarian snacks at home.

- Vegetarian school lunches can be easy to plan.

- Eating away from home can present difficulties sometimes for vegetarians. However, restaurants and fast-food places often have foods vegetarians can eat.

- Vegetarian teens can plan for snacks and meals away from home.

Chapter 6

Eating on the Go

Snacks Are Important

Snacks are important to all teens. They fuel the body with energy and provide nutrients for growth and health.

Vegetarian diets tend to be high in fiber. This nutrient can cause you to feel full quickly. Therefore, snacks can help vegetarian teens to get the nutrients they might miss if they get full fast at meals.

It's easy to keep good, tasty, and healthy snacks on hand. Dried fruits, trail mix, popcorn, pretzels, and cherry tomatoes are some you might try. Make a pizza with tofu, vegetables, cheese, or meat analogues. Then, eat slices later for snacks. Fill tacos or burritos with cooked beans, tofu, or vegetables. Heat some instant soup or spread bagels with sesame, almond, or peanut butter. These fun snacks can help to provide you with the nutrients and energy you need throughout the day.

At a Glance

Quick and easy power snacks:

Rice cakes with peanut butter and chopped carrots

Popcorn sprinkled with curry powder

Baked chips and salsa

Soy or dairy yogurt with nuts

Sliced apple and cheese sandwich

Peanut butter on an apple

Low-fat string cheese and crackers

Baby carrots with hummus

Smoothies on the Run

Ming, Age 16

Ming often makes a tofu smoothie for breakfast. She drinks it on her way to school. She found the recipe on the Internet.

When Amy slept over for the first time, Ming wasn't sure if Amy would want a smoothie. So she asked Amy before she made some.

"Sure. I'll have whatever you usually eat for breakfast," Amy said.

Ming got out the ingredients, and Amy helped her whip up a batch.

"This smoothie tastes really good," Amy said.

"I'm glad you like it," Ming replied. "The rest goes into the refrigerator. It's enough for another breakfast or two."

With planning, eating a vegetarian lunch at school isn't too hard.

Tofu Smoothie

Ingredients

1 box firm tofu (Use tofu in aseptic packs found on the grocery store shelf.)

½ cup (120 milliliters) fruit juice

3 tablespoons (45 grams) maple syrup or sugar to taste

At least ½ cup (115 milliliters) frozen fruit. (More fruit makes thicker smoothies.)

Vanilla or almond extract for flavor

Directions

Put all ingredients in a blender and blend until smooth. Makes three to four servings.

Lunches at School

A few vegetarian dishes may be on your school's lunch menu. Some teens choose to get lunch from their school's salad bar. They may add a sandwich or fruit brought from home.

Many vegetarian teens decide to bring their lunch to school. Planning ahead can make bringing your own lunch easy.

"A lot of times there's nothing I can eat if I go to the baseball stadium or a party. I just eat before I go or after I get home. It's not really fair to ask other people to adjust if I'm not willing to as well."—Peter, age 16

Fast Food and Restaurants

Connor, Age 14

Connor is vegan. One day he went with some friends to a fast-food restaurant for lunch. "What are the tortillas made of?" Connor asked the server.

"I don't know. I think just flour and water," the server said.

"Could you please find out? I don't eat dairy products, so I need to know."

The server went back to the kitchen. She came back and told Connor, "The flour tortillas contain whey, so they have dairy in them. But I found out that our taco chips, shells, and sauce don't have dairy in them."

"Thanks for checking," said Connor. "I'll have chips and salsa."

The demand for meatless meals is exploding. Vegetarians can sometimes find meatless items on a fast-food menu. But it's not always easy to tell if animal products are used in a food. Like Connor, ask the server if you're not sure about something on the menu.

Some restaurants can be vegetarian heaven. Many ethnic restaurants serve foods based on grains and vegetables. Most Japanese, Chinese, Thai, and Vietnamese restaurants have vegetarian meals as choices. Egyptian, Indian, and Mexican restaurants often do, too. You can check with any restaurant to see if vegetarian meals are on the menu. Call ahead and ask about vegetarian options. You even may be offered something that's not on the menu.

It's usually possible to eat vegetarian meals, even if you're not eating at home.

Tips for Eating Away From Home

Sometimes making a list can be helpful. You may want to write down some vegetarian meals that might be easy to get away from home. Remember such foods as vegetarian soups, salads, pasta salads, or baked potatoes.

Friends who invite you to eat with them may tell you what's for dinner. It's a good idea to let friends know ahead of time that you don't eat meat. But let them know that you like most other foods. You could offer a list of foods that you normally eat. This can make the task of providing a vegetarian meal seem less difficult. You might offer to bring a vegetarian dish to share.

Points to Consider

- What foods can a teen vegetarian eat at a party?

- What new healthy snacks are you willing to try?

- What role do snack foods play in your diet?

- Do you have any favorite restaurants? What foods do they have that are vegetarian?

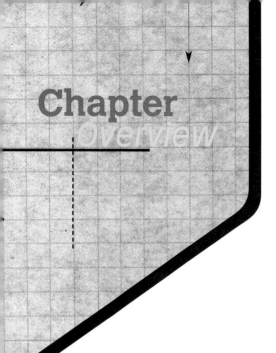

Chapter
Overview

- Family and friends may not always understand a teen's decision to become a vegetarian. By educating himself or herself, the teen can answer questions and explain his or her decision with confidence.

- Families can learn ways to make living with a vegetarian easy.

- People who become vegetarians can change their diet at their own pace.

- Vegetarianism is a personal choice.

Chapter 7

Making Vegetarianism Work for You

Dealing With Your Family and Friends

Vegetarianism is a healthy way of life when it's planned right. However, if you choose to become a vegetarian, family and friends sometimes may not understand your decision. Some people may not agree with the reasons or beliefs that lead you to vegetarianism. Some people may feel uncomfortable with your choice. They may feel that by becoming a vegetarian, you're judging their choice to eat meat or other animal foods. Your family may think that it takes extra work to feed a vegetarian. They may worry about your nutritional needs.

However, these things don't have to cause disagreements or misunderstandings. You can do three helpful things to ease your move to vegetarianism.

- Educate yourself and others. Learn the facts about vegetarianism and nutrition basics. Then you can handle questions with confidence.

- Do some of the grocery shopping and make some of your own meals.

- Respect other people's choices. Then they'll probably respect your choices, too.

Teen Talk

"Being a vegetarian hasn't been as hard as my family thought it would be. When my mom and sister eat hamburgers, I eat a veggie burger. In dishes that use meat, I use soy 'meat.' If I'm going to a party, my mom gives me a snack before I go."—Jess, age 13

"I help my dad make the shopping list, or we go shopping together. He's not vegetarian, but we can usually plan several meals a week that we both can eat. Otherwise, my dad just makes two versions of a recipe, one with meat and one without."—Betty, age 17

Anelia, Age 15

"I told my parents I was becoming a vegetarian for health reasons. My dad was interested and wanted to try it, too. He caved after three days, though. My mom wondered what she would cook. She worried that I wouldn't get enough protein and calcium. But I showed her some vegetarian articles I got on the Internet. She read the stuff about iron and vitamins in grains and beans. She was surprised, and now she trusts my choice a little more."

Making the Switch

Once you make the decision to become a vegetarian, learn as much as you can about vegetarian eating. This can help you make nutritious food choices. It can help your parents or guardians to trust your decision.

Families often find creative ways to live with a new vegetarian. Anelia's mom often prepares pasta and vegetables the whole family can eat. She also makes a meat dish for the meat eaters. The family shares a vegetarian dinner at least once a weck. Anelia sometimes helps to grocery shop to be sure that vegetarian food is on hand.

Teens who choose vegetarianism may have to help their family with the adjustment.

A Plan for Change

Some people suddenly trade their usual diet for a vegetarian one. Others may take their time making the switch. They may look for many new ways to meet their nutritional needs. The following tips can help you make the change.

- **Make a plan.** List the foods you normally eat. Mark the ones that are vegetarian. Start with these meals and build on them. Plan to eat several vegetarian meals each week with foods you know and like.

- **Add more vegetarian meals by leaving meat out of recipes.** Make chili with beans instead of beef. Use vegetables instead of beef in spaghetti sauce.

- **Try different products from the store.** Look for rice or grain mixes.

- **Make the dishes you usually do, but use meat substitutes.** Use tofu, seitan, or other meat substitutes instead of meat. These meat substitutes can ease the change to a vegetarian diet. Most supermarkets carry tofu and some meat substitutes in the produce section or the natural foods section. Check for veggie burgers, links, and patties in the frozen foods section. These foods are often near the breakfast foods.

Toby, Age 13

Toby has talked to his grandmother about being a vegetarian. His grandmother said she understood. "I will make you my special enchiladas without meat," she told him.

Yet at Toby's next visit, his grandmother handed him a filled plate. "Toby, I made my special beef enchiladas for you." Then she frowned. "I forgot that you don't eat meat!"

Toby unfolded his napkin. "That's no problem. I eat a hamburger sometimes when I'm out with friends. This is much better than that!"

Be patient with yourself if you change your diet. It's okay if you slip up and eat meat. You may not know the vegetable soup at lunch was cooked with chicken broth. Or you may not realize there's sausage on your pizza. Don't worry. After all, you control what you eat. Tomorrow you can make different choices.

Answering Questions

Your new diet can help you share a new world of experiences. People may ask why you made the choice to become a vegetarian. You can learn facts and plan good answers that are meaningful to you. You might share connections between food choices and health or environmental issues. If people joke about your vegetarianism, plan a funny reply. If people ask what you eat, tell them about new foods.

Most vegetarians see their diet as a celebration of food and life.

A Personal Choice

Vegetarianism is a personal choice. It may help people feel good about what they put into their body. It may be about following personal beliefs and making thoughtful decisions. Just remember that you can do whatever is comfortable for you. Even small steps can add up to good results.

Points to Consider

- What questions should a vegetarian be ready to answer? How would you answer these questions?

- Can you think of some times when you have changed your ideas about food? What caused these changes?

- What might be the hardest part about becoming a vegetarian?

- What are some benefits of vegetarian eating?

Internet Sites

International Vegetarian Union
www.ivu.org
Contains information about vegetarianism, animals and the environment, and famous vegetarians

Teen Vegetarian
www.geocities.com/HotSprings2657/
Has information about vegetarianism, vegetarian organizations, bands that are vegetarian, recipes, and lists of related sites

Vegetarian Nutrition for Teenagers
http://vegsoc.wellington.net.nz/teen.htm
Gives nutrition facts for vegetarian teens and lists other sites for vegetarian teens

Vegetarian Resource Group
www.vrg.org
Offers vegetarian and vegan recipes, nutrition information, and even a vegetarian game

The Vegetarian Youth Network
www.geocities.com/RainForest/Vines/4482
Gives reasons for vegetarianism and provides an e-mail list of other vegetarian teens you can contact

Veggie Sports Association
http://veggie.org
Provides information on how to be a healthy vegetarian athlete

Useful Addresses

American Dietetic Association (ADA)
National Center for Nutrition and Dietetics
216 West Jackson Boulevard
Chicago, IL 60606-6995
1-800-366-2655
www.eatright.org

American Vegan Society
56 Dinshah Lane
PO Box 369
Malaga, NJ 08328-0908

North American Vegetarian Society
PO Box 72
Dolgeville, NY 13329
www.navs-online.org

Toronto Vegetarian Association
2300 Yonge Street, Suite 1101
PO Box 2307
Toronto, ON M4P 1E4
CANADA
www.veg.on.ca

For Further Reading

Klaven, Ellen. *The Vegetarian Factfinder.* New York: Little Bookroom, 1996.

Krizmanic, Judy. *The Teen's Vegetarian Cookbook.* New York: Viking, 1999.

Parr, Jan. *The Young Vegetarian's Companion.* New York: Franklin Watts, 1996.

Pierson, Stephanie. *Vegetables Rock! A Complete Guide for Teenage Vegetarians.* New York: Bantam Books, 1999.

Glossary

analogue (AN-uh-log)—a meat substitute made from wheat or soy

fiber (FYE-bur)—a part of plant foods that aids in food digestion

hummus (HUH-muhss)—a paste made from chickpeas that is often used as a dip or sandwich spread

lacto-ovo vegetarian (LAC-toh-OH-voh vej-uh-TER-ee-uhn)—a person who eats eggs and dairy products as well as plant foods, but no meat

lacto vegetarian (LAC-toh vej-uh-TER-ee-uhn)—a person who eats plant foods and dairy products but no meat or eggs

ovo vegetarian (OH-voh vej-uh-TER-ee-uhn)—a person who eats plant foods and eggs but no dairy products or meat

nutrient (NOO-tree-uhnt)—a substance in food that helps keep the body strong and healthy

seitan (SAY-tahn)—a meatlike food made from wheat flour to take the place of chicken, beef, or pork in cooking

tempeh (TEM-pay)—a dense meat substitute patty made from soybeans

tofu (TOH-foo)—a soft, cheeselike food made from soybeans

TVP (TEE-vee-pee)—stands for textured vegetable protein, a meat substitute made from soy flour

vegan (VEE-guhn)—a vegetarian who eats no animal or dairy products

vegetarian (vej-uh-TER-ee-uhn)—a person who eats mostly plant foods; some vegetarians eat poultry and fish, but no red meat; some may not eat any animal products.

vegetarianism (vej-uh-TER-ee-uhn-iz-uhm)—the practice of vegetarian eating and lifestyle

Index

Index